Growing your own food is like printing your own money.

Buckwheat, beet, green pea, and radish sprouts

I love sprouts! I love growing them, caring for them, seeing their brilliant colors and harvesting them. I love having shelves in my kitchen window that overflow with life and a fridge full of fresh sprouts, ready to be tossed with other veggies to make a delicious, colorful and life-filled meal.

I also love teaching others to do the same—to demonstrate how easy it can be to have one's very own kitchen sprout garden, with fresh food to enjoy in less than 48 hours.

One of the most empowering things we can do is to grow our own food. Growing a garden in the yard is a privilege and treat that grows and flows with the seasons, and often depends upon us actually having the time and access to a soft bed of earth to plant the seeds.

What I love about sprouts is that the growing season is year-round, and I have to wait only 2–10 days to enjoy my harvest. These little lovelies can grow no matter what the weather, space constraints or growing conditions.

Once we have a bit of knowledge and a simple system in place, we can grow our sprouts and be assured of the freshness and quality of our food. It's comforting to know that we have the absolute best organic, living and nutrient-rich food on the planet—right in our very own kitchen.

You can begin by building some simple shelves in a window, clearing a space on the countertop or finding a hook to hang your sprout bag from.

Decide upon a few types of beans or seeds to get started with, and experiment a bit. Soon you'll be expanding your growing system and your delicious harvest.

In no time at all you'll have a dozen or more different types of sprouts growing happily all over your kitchen, adding outstanding nutrition, variety and color to every meal. Have the kids join in, bring a tray of greens to a friend as a quick gift, and share your beautiful bounty. How sweet is that?

Enjoy the journey!

Linda

Radish Sprouts

What Is a Sprout?

Sprouts are the most energy-rich and nutrient-packed foods that you can possibly consume. Sprouts are the babies of any bean, seed or grain that has been brought to life by soaking in water. Seeds, beans, nuts and grains will remain in a dormant state virtually forever until they are brought to life with one simple action: the addition of water.

Soaking a dormant seed, bean, nut or grain in water removes the enzyme inhibitor, which keeps it protected and sleeping until the water awakens it to life.

Once that process has started, enzymes become the catalyst that turn the seed into a mature plant.

These powerful enzymes are the basis of the "Living Foods" approach to a vibrant and healthy diet. The more "living" a food is (meaning that it is still in a growing state such as a sprout or has not been heated over 105 degrees) the more this life force and enzyme activity is available to keep all the systems of your heavenly body in the healthiest state possible.

So consume fresh sprouts at every meal; eat them plain; eat them fancy; add them to your smoothies and juices, and combine them with other delicious veggies for a knock-out salad meal. You can't get any fresher than this!

TABLE OF CONTENTS

Sunflower Sprouts

Soup & Sandwich Ideas (Continued)

Salad Ideas

Desserts

Gift Ideas for Sharing

Resources

THIS IS ACTUALLY EASY!

Starting your kitchen garden

Growing sprouts is actually very easy once you get started. They are pre-programed to grow; so, from the moment you have added that magic ingredient, water, there is not much you can do to stop them or mess it up. Spend a few minutes a day to keep them rinsed and watered, add a bit of love and attention, and voila! You've Got Sprouts!

Start with good quality organic seeds, beans, nuts and grains. Start small so that you can evaluate your harvest and determine which tastes you enjoy the most, and the growing methods you prefer. There are truly dozens of possibilities! So get creative and seek out new seeds regularly for a variety of tastes and optimal nutritional value.

As for growing containers and systems, I have tried many different sprouting gadgets, machines, tools and tricks, and I always come back to the basic methods that are demonstrated in the book, and in our DVD, Homegrown to homemade.

Visit www.HealthyEasyGreen.com for purchase.

Once your harvest comes in, you'll want to write down your new recipes and taste experiments as well.

Depending upon the size of your family and the rate that you consume the different sprouts, you will also discover how often you'll need to start new batches. I find that I can start a new batch every 2-4 days to have a continual supply of fresh sprouts on my shelves, on my counter and in my fridge.

At first, your sprouts may surprise you by growing twice as much as you had expected, so don't forget to share your extra harvest with your friends. They will be thrilled to eat them and inspired to begin growing their own. The joy and pride of having a kitchen garden is contagious!

So jump in, and let's begin!

Soaking seeds, beans, nuts and grains

Getting Started

Here are the basic techniques to get your kitchen garden started. The easiest way to begin, giving you the best variety of sprouts, is with jars, sprout bags and soil-filled trays. Check out our Resource section for sprouting materials, seeds and soil, plus our hour-long instructional video, *Homegrown to Homemade*.

With all your sprouting choices and recipe ingredients, don't forgot to choose organic; it's the best for you and the planet!

Sprouting in Jars

With a screen over the opening of a wide-mouth jar:

SEEDS: Soak overnight approximately 2 tablespoons of the small seeds; my favorite seeds are clover, alfalfa, broccoli, fenugrec and radish.

BEANS: Soak 3-4 tablespoons of the most common legumes used for sprouting which are lentils, mung and aduki beans, green peas and chick peas.

In the morning, drain and rinse 3 to 4 times with fresh water, then place at an angle to drain. Repeat the same routine in the evening.

They are ready when the tails are as long as the bean, in about 48 hours.

The small "leafy" sprouts such as alfalfa, clover and broccoli are ready in 4-5 days when their first little leaves appear.

Rinse and drain well one last time before storing in the fridge in their jar with the cap on. You can also store in Green Bags with a paper towel to pull in any extra moisture. Placing them in the fridge will slow down their growth, and they'll remain fresh for another 4-6 days. If properly rinsed and drained, they don't need to be rinsed again before serving.

Sprouting with a Sprout Bag

Any type of bean, nut, seed or grain can be sprouted in a fine mesh Sprout Bag (see Resource section for purchase). Sprout Bags are awesome for travel because you can soak, rinse, drain, grow and store all of your sprouts while on the road, without any bulky equipment. They're easy to use in a hotel room or while away from home for a period of time.

I like to sprout my buckwheat and quinoa in sprout bags. It seems better this way so I can rinse them by gently massaging them, in the bag, under a continuous spray of cool water. These two types of grains release a glutinous residue when soaking and sprouting, so extra rinsing is a good thing to guarantee their freshness.

When your sprouts are rinsed well, suspend the bag from the cupboard handle or a hook, and let drain completely. Once they are well drained, place the bag of your sprouting babies in an empty bowl to keep some of the moisture in, and let them rest until the next rinsing.

Repeat the cycle; rinse well, drain and rest until they are ready to be added into a recipe or stored in the fridge. Buckwheat and quinoa take about 48 hours to reach this stage, as well as the beans. The smaller sprouts, such as clover, broccoli and alfalfa, take 4 to 5 days to grow their beautiful tiny leaves.

12

Tray Sprouts

Soak your favorite beans and seeds overnight. My favorite tray sprouts are sunflower, pea, buckwheat and wheatgrass.

Spread a layer of your soaked seeds on top of moist organic top soil or potting soil. The seeds should touch, but not overlap.

The seeds grow well when they have a bit of pressure on them for the first 48 hours, so you can stack your trays by placing another soil-filled tray on top, or to finish the stack, an empty tray with a light weight on it, another soil-filled tray or a jar of water.

Once your sprouts have taken hold of the soil with a small root reaching downward and a small shoot reaching upward, it's time to un-stack them, lay them out on their shelves and let them grow.

Water with a light spray once a day if there are no drainage holes in the bottoms, and twice a day if there are drain holes. Basically, keep an eye on them and water as needed, making sure the soil is moist but not wet or retaining any pooled water. If you have watered too much and there are no holes in the bottom of your trays to drain, just tilt the tray a bit over the sink and let the water drain off. Direct sun is hard on them, so choose a spot close to a northern or eastern window if possible or draw a light curtain over a southerly window if that's your best option. You can also use full-spectrum grow lights.

In 7-10 days, your sprouts will be ready to harvest by cutting them at their base with a sharp knife. There should be no need to wash them; they can go directly into a bag and stored in the fridge, where they'll keep for 4-6 days.

14

Washing Your Little Sprouts
For The Freshest Harvest

When it comes to the little sprouts, such as broccoli, clover and alfalfa, I give them an extra washing to have the freshest sprouts possible. It's worth the extra care! Your sprouts will last for days if you take this extra little step. Sprouts are fine to eat with the hulls on them, but I feel they taste fresher and last longer if I remove them before storing them in the fridge.

Fill a large bowl with fresh cool water, and put your sprouts in it. Swirl and shake them gently in the water, and you'll see the sprouted hulls wash away from your sprouts and float to the surface. Skim these off and discard. Swirl some more and continue to skim off any floating hulls until there are very few left.

With your salad spinner nearby, gently lift your sprouts straight out of the water. You'll see the un-sprouted seeds have settled to the bottom, so avoid catching any of them. Place your sprouts in the spinner, and gently spin to remove excess water.

Spread your rinsed and spun sprouts onto a clean cotton dishcloth, and cover lightly with plastic wrap to keep the delicate roots from drying out. Don't close the edges; you'll want some air to access them.

Leave on the counter for a few hours. They will green-up with that last bit of light-produced chlorophyll.

Place them on a paper towel in a glass or clear plastic container, and store in the fridge. They are now ready to eat straight out of the container. No need to wash or rinse again before serving. Now that's easy food prep!

Clover Sprouts

Wheatgrass Juice

Wheatgrass has earned its reputation as the "ultimate juice." Health-conscious people around the world are downing shots of wheatgrass to reverse and prevent illness and age-related decline. With a nutritional profile off the charts, wheatgrass juice offers a sublime pick-me up, delivers serious health repair and is an outstanding preventative natural medicine of choice.

Just two ounces, twice a day, can help you improve your overall health, from top to bottom, by fortifying the blood with amazing sun-filled chlorophyll. With a molecular structure nearly identical to hemoglobin (that which carries oxygen to the cells), the living blood of this grass carries liquid oxygen to our cells and rejuvenates our blood as well.

Wheatgrass offers a complete vitamin and mineral profile along with trace elements and life-sustaining enzymes. If that wasn't enough, it is a rich source of protein, containing 17 amino acids—the building blocks of protein.

A two-ounce shot of wheatgrass is an intense drink that goes down well with a squeeze of lemon or followed by a swish of cool water. It is best taken on an empty stomach. It is an acquired taste, so start out with one ounce and build up to two ounces, once or twice a day. You will be positively glowing in no time!

Invest in a good juicer that will extract the juice from the grass. If you aren't going to be growing it yourself, you can find local sources that can provide your grass and have it delivered right to your door. Visit our resource page for some suggestions of growers who offer wheatgrass and juicers.

Green Juices

The juice of green leafy vegetables contains a powerhouse of wonderful chlorophyll and a garden full of vitamins and minerals. An 8- to 16-ounce glass of green juice is alkalizing and refreshing as a meal in itself or great for a mid-day pick-me-up. Green juices offer pure nutrition without the sugar of fruit juices that can often cause swings in our blood sugar levels.

All organic green leafy vegetables are a great addition for your juice; some common choices are kale, chard, romaine lettuce, sunflower, pea and buckwheat sprouts, spinach and more.

Add celery and cucumber to give volume and freshness, and follow with parsley, cilantro or a branch or two of other fresh herbs.

I love adding the juice of half a lemon and an inch of ginger juice to keep it fresh. A clove of garlic gives it the final touch for a delicious life-giving juice.

Ideally, consume your juice within 20 minutes of making it, but if you want to preserve some for later, adding lemon and keeping the juice very cold will help keep it tasty throughout the day. Take some to the office with you in a thermos with a bit of ice for freshness.

Left: HIPPOCRATES GREEN JUICE

For 16 ounces, juice 50% sunflower and pea sprouts and 50% celery and cucumber. 2 cups sunflower, 2 cups peas, 1 cucumber and 3 celery stalks.

Center: PURE CUCUMBER JUICE

Wash and juice 3 or 4 organic cucumbers for a refreshing mid-morning drink; it's a delicious way to begin your day.

Right: GORGEOUS GREEN JUICE

Start by juicing 2 kale leaves and handful each of spinach, sunflower and pea sprouts. Juice a few leaves of crisp romaine lettuce, and follow with 2 cucumbers and 3 sticks of celery.

Half a lemon with an inch of ginger and a clove of garlic will round it out if you want to vary the taste.

Sprouted Seed Waters

Any seed, nut, bean or grain that has been soaked is considered a "sprout."

The enzyme inhibitor has been soaked away, and that seed has come alive.

I enjoy adding chia or flax seeds to my water bottle that I drink and consume throughout the day.

I start with a base of liquid; fresh baby coconut water is my absolute favorite when I am fortunate to get it fresh. Second best is the coconut water in cartons that are sold in nearly every health food store and grocery. These have been pasteurized to extend their shelf life, so the enzyme content is absent, but they are a suitable second-best alternative.

Pure or alkaline water makes a delicious base as well.

To your liquid base, add about 2 inches of chia or flax seed to your bottle (I prefer glass over plastic), then add your liquid. Let this soak for a few hours. The seeds become gelatinous and thicken the water slightly.

You can add a teaspoon of organic fruit concentrate liquid, found bottled in most health food stores, for extra flavor. Blueberry, raspberry and cranberry are some of the common fruit concentrates that you'll find.

As you drink, give the bottle a little swirl with each sip, and then the seeds are easy to swallow or crunch. It's refreshing and filling.

Smoothies

Smoothies are the easiest and quickest way to consume sprouts on the go. There are countless variations of smoothies; they can be based with green veggies or with fruits. Whatever the combo, they offer concentrated, delicious nutrition in minutes. Try inventing your own combo!

Here are two of my favorites:

GREEN SMOOTHIE

Start with 2 cups of liquid; this can be pure water or freshly juiced cucumber, celery or carrot juice.

Add 2 leaves of Kale (I remove the stem) or other leafy green, a handful of each kind of sprout I may have on hand (sunflower, pea and buckwheat are my favorites), a few tablespoons of broccoli or clover sprouts, a cucumber cut in 2"pieces, a green apple and a squeeze of lemon. I finish with a drizzle of omega-rich oil such as hemp, chia or flax. Blend in a powerful blender such as a Vitamix. A less powerful type of blender will do the trick as well; it just might not be as smooth as from the Vitamix.

BUCKWHEAT AND FRUIT SMOOTHIE

In a base of 2 cups liquid such as rice milk or half water and half fruit juice, add a cup of fruit. Mango is a favorite of mine, either fresh or frozen, but you can use pear, apple, berries or whatever you have on hand. Add 1/2 cup sprouted buckwheat and/or sprouted quinoa and blend. A sprinkle of cinnamon or nutmeg makes it extra tasty.

Superfood concentrates add an extra boost to the nutritional value of your smoothies. I often use my smoothies to carry some of my liquid and powder supplements. Here are some superfoods that I add to each smoothie; try one spoonful of any of the following: maca, lecithin, bee pollen, blue-green algae, camu powder (vit C), and a spoonful of an omega-rich oil such as hemp or flax oil. I then add some of my less-than-delicious vitamin drops such as silica, vitamin D or mineral concentrates. These don't alter the taste of the smoothie, but add a super charge of nutrition. Visit www.HealthyEasyGreen.com for providers.

Sprouted Almond or Buckwheat Milk

Sprouted almond or buckwheat milk is easy to prepare and great to have on hand for a refreshing drink or addition to a recipe.

Soak 2 cups of almonds or buckwheat groats (the white hulled buckwheat) for at least 6 hours or overnight. Rinse and drain well, and place in a blender with two to three times the water. Twice the water will give you a creamy milk, and three times the water will give you a consistency of a 2% milk. Blend at high speed until well blended, about 30-60 seconds.

Place a mesh sprout bag over a large bowl or measuring cup that has a spout on it, and pour the milk mixture into it. With clean hands, lift the bag and gently begin to twist and squeeze the bag until all the liquid is out and only the pulp remains. Store the milk in jars in the fridge for 4-5 days. The pulp can be used for cookies and crackers.

BREAKFAST IDEAS

CREAM OF SPROUTED BUCKWHEAT

This creamy treat is a welcome breakfast on a chilly morning.

1 cup liquid
(water or milk such as rice, buckwheat or almond milk; page 25)

2 tsp Omega-rich oil such as flax or hemp

1 cup sprouted buckwheat, or 50/50 mix of sprouted buckwheat and quinoa

Pinch of nutmeg and cinnamon, to taste

Blend all in blender. To warm, place in saucepan and stir over low heat until your finger tells you the mixture is warm. If it's too hot for your finger, you risk destroying the beneficial enzymes. Pour into small bowls. Garnish with a few slices of banana and a drizzle of maple syrup if you need added sweetness (I prefer it without), and top off with a sprinkle of cinnamon and serve.

Serves 2

MUESLI MIX

This mixture can be so versatile; use the grains, nuts, seeds and fruits you have on hand, and you can never go wrong with this nutritious cereal base. Here is the basic idea:

Mix together in a large bowl.

2 cups of grain flakes. This can be a combination of any or all of the following; oats, rye, kamut, millet or spelt.
(These are not to be of the quick-cooking variety, but the large flakes.)

1/4 cup each of any or all of the following seeds and nuts:
chopped walnuts and pecans, pumpkin, flax, chia, hemp, sesame or sunflower seeds.
Steel cut oats are a great addition as well.

1/4 cup each of any of the following dried fruits:
cranberries, goji berries, blueberries or raisins.

1/4 cup of unsweetened coconut.

Mix thoroughly and store in jars until ready to use.

Chia Pudding

Chia pudding is an easy and fun dish to make and eat. The soaked chia seeds are smooth and crunchy at the same time. Use either the dark or light seeds, or mix them together. Here are two ways to prepare it; you can invent more variations. This amount makes one portion, so multiply your quantities and number of bowls per person. Any leftover pudding can be spread on a Teflex sheet in the dehydrator to make crunchy little sweet crackers.

APPLE AND BLUEBERRY CHIA

In each individual small bowl, pour 3/4 cup of apple juice. Stir in 1/4 cup of chia seeds and a pinch of cinnamon, and let soak for at least 10 minutes. Garnish with fresh blueberries, a sprinkle of hemp seeds and serve. (May not be as smooth as from the Vitamix.)

COCONUT AND NUT MILK CHIA

In each individual small bowl, pour 3/4 cup of almond milk, buckwheat milk or rice milk. Stir in 1/4 cup of chia seeds and a pinch of nutmeg. Let soak for at least 10 minutes. Garnish with unsweetened shredded coconut and small chunks of fresh strawberries.

Before consuming, add more liquid if needed to create the consistency you prefer; it gels up the longer it soaks.

BREAKFAST MUESLI

Prepare this recipe before going to bed:

Place 1/2 cup of the mixture into individual small bowls, and cover with liquid just to the top of the grains. This will begin the sprouting process and bring your cereal to life. The liquid can be water or a mixture of half water and half apple juice. For a really sweet cereal, cover with undiluted apple juice.

Place a small plate over the bowl and let it soak overnight. In the morning you`ll have a delicious soaked cereal that is filled with beautiful fruit colors and a load of nutrition. Add a bit more liquid if needed, and garnish with grated fresh apple.

Delicious!

Dehydrated Buckwheat Sprouts (Buckwheaties)

Sprouted and dehydrated buckwheat groats are a versatile staple to have on hand. Plain or spiced up, they are a crunchy snack as is, or can be enjoyed as a breakfast cereal with buckwheat milk (see page 25). They add variety and crunch to salads, cookies, snacks and desserts.

Soak 2 cups hulled buckwheat groats for at least 6 hours or overnight in a sprout bag. Rinse well and drain morning and night. Let them sprout for 24 hours, or until a small tail begins to grow. Rinse extra well and drain once more, then spread onto a dehydrator tray. At this point you can sweeten them up by tossing with a couple of drops of Stevia and a shake of cinnamon, or spice them with herbs and cayenne for a zesty salad sprinkle. Dehydrate at 105 degrees for 12 hours, or until very crunchy.

Stores in a glass jars indefinitely.

EMERALD SUNFLOWER AND AVOCADO SOUP

This beautifully creamy soup is a favorite of all. Rich and velvety, full of protein and green sunshine, it is an all-around experience to enjoy.

IN A BLENDER, MIX:

2 large or 3 small avocados
1 cup spinach leaves
1 cup sunflower sprouts
2 Tbsp chopped cilantro leaves
2 Tbsp lemon juice (about 1/2 lemon)
1 clove garlic, crushed
1 inch ginger, grated
1 tsp dulse or kelp powder, or herbal salt
1 pinch cayenne pepper

Fill the blender with all the ingredients except the liquid (water, cucumber juice or coconut water). Fill the blender with liquid to about half the level of the ingredients. Blend and add more liquid slowly until desired consistency. Serve in small bowls (this is a rich soup; large portions are not needed), and garnish with chopped red pepper and a cilantro leaf.

Serves 4

MISO SOUP

This is an easy and satisfying soup, made in minutes. A yellow miso is mellower, and the red or dark brown miso will be saltier. Be sure not to boil the miso paste or you will lose the beneficial enzymes.

In a medium saucepan, bring 4 cups of water to a boil, then reduce to a simmer.

Add any or all of the following variety of veggies, chopped in large pieces:

1 stem of Broccoli fleurettes

1/2 zucchini sliced thick

A dozen or so tender baby asparagus, cut in 1 inch pieces

5 or 6 mushrooms cut in half

2 or 3 baby Bok Choy sliced lengthwise

2 green onions,
cut in inch-long diagonal pieces

1 clove chopped garlic

1/2 inch grated ginger

1/2 sheet Nori seaweed, cut into thin strips

1 tsp herbal salt or dulse flakes

3 Tbsp miso paste

Let the veggies simmer 4 to 5 minutes, just until they are tender but still brilliant green. Add 1 cup white bean sprouts and a handful of mung bean sprouts. Cover the pan and turn off the heat. Let the bean sprouts become tender while you mix the following in a small bowl: 3 Tbsp water and 3 Tbsp miso paste. Stir until blended, and pour into the soup mix. Gently stir the whole soup and serve while the sprouts are still crunchy.

Makes 2 large meal soups or
4 smaller portions

Sandwiches and Wraps

Sandwiches and wraps are a quick way to enjoy your sprouts, and the combinations are endless.

I like to start with a good sprouted bread or wrap. You can wrap your mixes in a sprouted grain wrap, or a collard green leaf or Nori sheet. I mix and match that with whatever is growing on my sprout shelf or harvested in my fridge. Some of my favorite base spreads are a good hummus or the Spicy Almond Butter dressing, while the veggie combos can include cucumbers, avocados, tomatoes or roasted Portobello mushrooms and red peppers. Top that with sunflower sprouts, buckwheat lettuce or pea.

To spice it up, finish with radish sprouts or broccoli and clover. Drizzle a bit of tangy salad dressing to keep it juicy, and either top with the second slice of bread or roll it all in a wrap.

Totally delicious!

Sprouted Nori Wrap

Small leafy sprouts such as clover, alfalfa and broccoli go well in Nori rolls. Nori is the seaweed used to make sushi. There are many variations of Nori rolls; this is the basic ingredient suggestion.

Lay the nori sheet out on a flat surface and spread the following ingredients across the width of one end of the sheet: a nice mound of sprouts about an inch high; 2 asparagus; a thinly cut carrot strip; thin slices of red pepper; a green onion sliced down the middle; and thin pieces of avocado.

Roll tightly and moisten the end of the Nori to have it stick together. Cut with a sharp serrated knife and arrange on plate. Serve with Nama Shoyu, wasabi and sliced ginger.

SALAD IDEAS

SIMPLE GRAIN AND SPROUTED BEAN BOWL

This is one of my easy favorites. Freshly cooked grain such as millet, quinoa or rice offer a great base for this quick and hearty salad. In this example, I have cooked organic rice and sprouted mung beans.

To prepare, in each bowl, place your grain (slightly warmed if you like), then add your favorite sprouted bean or bean mix. Serve with a Spicy Almond Dressing (page 53), and you've got a delicious and filling meal in a bowl. So simple!

PURE & FRESH SALAD

This is so easy. It's a joy to serve as a quick, refreshing entrée.

On a bed of sunflower or buckwheat sprouts, add a few mesclun salad leaves, a few shaved slices of purple cabbage for a splash of color, and top with a ring of sweet purple onion. The simplest of vinaigrettes is the best way to top this off: a drizzle of organic olive oil and a squeeze of fresh lemon juice.

Simply delicious.

Make It a Meal Salad

I love going around my kitchen to collect my fresh sprout harvest. I gather a few snips of garlic chive or radish and beet sprouts growing in the window, a handful of tall buckwheat, sunflower and pea, a shake of bean sprouts from their jars, and a portion of fluffy, silky clover, broccoli and alfalfa sprouts from the fridge. The weather outside can be frightful, but I have my fresh colorful harvest right beside my counter. Sweet!

This total meal salad is the easiest and most delicious way to get your variety of sprouts at every meal. This is where you'll be glad to have your sunny sprouts growing all over your kitchen.

To serve, begin by layering your largest sprouts on the plate; sprouts such as buckwheat lettuce, sunflower and pea greens. Then, I like to form a little nest in the center made of clover, broccoli and/or alfalfa sprouts, in which I place my fenugreek and sprouted beans. These can be a mix of mung beans, lentils, aduki beans and/or chick peas. In the very center, place a bouquet of radish or beet sprouts, and voilá! You have a complete meal, with all the benefits of outrageous color, life-force and vitality, not to mention the outstanding profile of vitamins, minerals, phytonutrients and amino acids.

In a large bowl, combine the following veggies:

1/2 cup broccoli fleurettes

1/4 cup sprouted mung beans

1 large kale leaf, chopped fine

1 cup spinach leaves, slightly chopped

1 cup sunflower sprouts, the top inch or so only

1/4 cup sunflower seeds

Toss with Asian dressing (page 54); garnish with a nest of "Spiralized" zucchini and sunflower tops. You can also use a Mandolin tool to achieve the thin zucchini.

Serve on a bed of whole spinach leaves, kale leaf and cucumber slices.

Serves 2-4

SUNNY CARROT AND BEET SALAD

In a bowl, place:

2 cups of finely shredded carrots

1 chopped green onion

1/4 cup sesame seeds

Toss with a simple vinaigrette of olive oil and lemon juice. Mound the carrots on a plate, and cover with cut baby beet sprouts. Finish with a sprinkle of sesame seeds and serve.

Serves 2

In this salad, I chopped various veggies from my garden and my fridge. Use what you have on hand, but here is the basic idea. It's easy and quick! In the base of salad greens of any kind, I added chopped Chinese cabbage, chopped sunflower and pea sprout tops and crispy cucumber. To give it a final crunch, you can add a chopped slice of onion, corn cut freshly right off the cobb, half a chopped sweet red bell pepper and a few sliced green olives. Top that with a Spicy Almond Butter Dressing (page 53), and you've got yourself a delicious meal in a bowl.

ALMOND AND BEAN SPROUT SALAD

I love this little green salad. The long white crunchy bean sprouts we know as "chop suey" are actually sprouted mung beans that are grown under pressure and in darkness for 7-10 days. It is a great complement to the baby mung bean sprouts that take 48 hours to grow.

In this salad, mix equal parts of broccoli florettes, chopped baby asparagus, pea sprout tops, sprouted mung beans and "chop suey" bean sprouts. Sprinkle generously with sliced almonds, and toss with an Asian Sesame Dressing (page 54).

ASPARAGUS AND LENTIL SALAD

It's easy to add sprouts to enhance every salad. Here is a simply satisfying salad of crunchy veggies and lentils.

Mix 2 cups of sliced baby asparagus and 2 cups chopped red and yellow peppers. Add 4 Tbsp of chopped red onion and 1/2 cup sprouted lentils. Serve on a bed of greens with a simple oil and lemon dressing.

SPICY SPROUTED MIXED BEAN SALAD

2 cups sprouted bean mix
(chick pea, lentil, aduki, mung, pea)

1/2 sweet red pepper chopped

2 slices of red onion, chopped

Large handful of parsley, chopped

One sliced green onion

Mix all ingredients in bowl and toss until creamy with Spicy Almond Butter Dressing (page 53). Serve on a bed of greens as a side salad, or roll into your favorite wrap mixture.

Serves 2 to 4

SPICY ALMOND BUTTER DRESSING AND PATÉ

This versatile paté can be used thinly as a salad dressing or thicker as a spread on sandwiches and wraps. When left overnight in the fridge, it does thicken up somewhat, so use it as a spread as is or add one spoonful of water at a time, stirring until the desired consistency. Makes about 3/4 cup of dressing.

In blender, mix together the following ingredients. Add water, then slowly add more, just until the mixture turns smoothly in the blender having a consistency of pancake batter:

2 Tbsp lemon juice or half a lemon

1/2 cup almond butter, raw or roasted

1 tsp freshly grated ginger

1 large clove garlic, crushed

2 pinches of cayenne or chipotle cayenne pepper to taste

1 Tbsp Braggs or Nama Shoyu

1/4 cup water

For the Asian and Italian dressings, mix the ingredients in a large measuring cup, then pour into a nice decorative bottle that will keep for a couple of weeks in the fridge.

ASIAN SESAME DRESSING

1 1/2 cups sesame oil

2 Tbsp toasted sesame oil

1/4 cup lemon juice

1 Tbsp orange juice

1 Tbsp Braggs or Nama Shoyu

1/4 cup sesame seeds

1/2 tsp herbal salt or dulse

1 Tbsp grated ginger

1 large clove garlic, crushed

1 pinch cayenne pepper

ITALIAN STYLE DRESSING

In a large mixing cup, combine:

1 cup olive oil

3 Tbsp lemon juice

I large or 2 small cloves crushed garlic

2 Tbsp dried parsley

1 tsp dried oregano

1 tsp dried basil

1/4 tsp dried thyme

1/2 tsp celery powder

1/2 tsp salt or
1 tsp dulse flakes

Pinch cayenne pepper

54

Email Linda@HealthyEasyGreen.com for the Stevia (Sugar-free) version of the following desserts.

MUESLI CRUNCH COOKIES

These action-packed cookies can also be made into bars for a homemade power/granola bar. The base of this recipe is the Muesli Mix recipe.

Soak 2 cups Muesli mix (page 30) in 1 cup apple or pear juice for an hour or so.

Mix well with:
Juice of 1/2 lemon
1 tsp vanilla extract
1/4 cup maple syrup
1/2 tsp each of cinnamon and nutmeg
2 Tbsp chia seeds
2 Tbsp psyllium powder

With a tablespoon measure, scoop the mixture and form into balls. Place on dehydrator tray and press slightly. Dehydrate at 105 degrees for 12 – 18 hours, depending on how chewy you like them. If you'd like power bars, form a 1/2 " deep square with the mixture on a Teflex sheet, and gently score into rectangles. Halfway through the dehydrating process, turn the mix over onto the dehydrator screen, and continue until the desired finish. Store in a sealed container in the fridge.

Makes about 18 cookies or 12 bars

KATHARINE'S FUDGE

My good friend Katharine Clark shared this recipe with me, and I've made it dozens of times since. It is so easy to prepare and is a great gift to give as well. Just be sure to keep your chocolates cool or in the fridge when not enjoying them as the coconut oils in the recipe will soften. It's so much better when they melt in your mouth! They are totally decadent, but surprisingly healthy.

You'll need a flexible mold of some sort; you need to gently twist the mold with the hardened chocolate to pop it out, so glass does not work. A rectangular plastic food storage container is a perfect mold for the "chocolate bar," and silicone molds that deliver chocolates in the shape of hearts is also fun. You can find these in a kitchen supply store.

In a large measuring cup or bowl with a spout (so you can pour into the molds), blend the following liquid ingredients until smooth:

1/3 cup liquid coconut oil

1/3 cup softened coconut butter

1/3 cup maple syrup

1 tsp vanilla

Sift 1 cup raw cacao or carob powder over the mixture and blend it all. Katharine likes to add 1 tbsp of Blue Green Algae to the mix at this point to give it an extra boost of green power. It blends perfectly so you don't get any algae taste. Check out the Resources section for Blue Green Algae.

Sprinkle sprouted and dehydrated buckwheat groats on the bottom of the molds, then pour the liquid chocolate mixture over it all. Freeze for 30 minutes, then un-mold and store in the fridge. Makes 12-15 chocolate hearts or 2 rectangular bars. If you don't have dehydrated buckwheat, use chopped walnuts or pecans if you'd like it crunchy, or leave them out for a creamy result.

SPROUTED ALMOND KEY LIME PIE

Pie:

2 1/2 cups almonds soaked overnight

3/4 cup lime juice

3/4 cup liquefied coconut oil

3/4 cup maple syrup

1 tsp vanilla

1 tsp grated lime peel

Crust:

2 cups nuts or mix of nuts such as almonds, walnuts or pecans

16 pitted Medjool dates

For the crust, grind nuts to a powder in food processor with the S blade. Add pitted dates and process until the mixture sticks together when pressed into a ball. Cover the bottom of the spring form pan with dried shredded coconut and press the date/nut mixture evenly and firmly on the bottom.

For the pie, rinse and drain the soaked and sprouted almonds. In a pot of simmering water, drop the almonds and stir for 60 seconds. Drain again and put the almonds into a bowl of very cold water. The skins will now pop off when you squeeze them. Do the squeezing into your opposite hand as they do become like little missiles and can shoot across the kitchen.
Put the almonds and the balance of the ingredients into a high powered blender like a Vitamix, and blend until very creamy.

Pour over the crust mixture and freeze for 3 hours or until completely firm. Remove from spring pan onto a flat plate, and keep refrigerated. Garnish with lime slices or berries prior to serving.

CRISPY CHIA SEED COOKIES

1/4 cup chia seeds

3/4 cup almond, rice, buckwheat milk, or coconut water

1/4 cup maple syrup

2 Tbsp liquefied coconut oil

1 tsp vanilla

1/2 tsp coriander

1/2 tsp cinnamon

1/3 cup shredded coconut

Mix chia seeds, your choice of milk or coconut water (you can also use fruit juice for a different taste), maple syrup, coconut oil and vanilla. Let soak for 15 minutes or so, and add more liquid if needed to obtain a thick but pourable mixture. Add spices and shredded coconut. Pour small rounds onto the Teflex sheet of a dehydrator and flatten. Dehydrate for 8 hours or until they peel from the sheet, then flip them onto the screen and continue a few hours until they are crispy. Stores for weeks in an airtight container.

The Gift of Life

Sharing sprouts is like sharing the gift of life. I have different sizes of trays in which I grow my sprouts, and I always like growing a variety in smaller trays: sized 5 x 8 or similar. That way, if I am running off to meet a friend, or am invited to have supper at someone's house, I have a sweet little gift to offer them to say I cherish their friendship. It`s always a welcome gift, and it gets them interested in growing their own, too.

Sprouts will grow virtually in any container, so get creative and have some fun! Take-out trays with their covers is an easy way to offer sprouts for the kitchen. For a more decorative touch, try growing wheatgrass, buckwheat or colorful beet sprouts in cute bowls, boxes or other containers. They make great centerpieces for events, even weddings. Keep a tray of wheatgrass in your office for a bit of an oxygen boost and pretty green sunshine.

Beet Sprouts

Broccoli, wheatgrass and beet sprouts

MY FAVORITE SPROUTING SEEDS

Small Leafy Green Sprouts (Jars Or Sprout Bags)

- Red clover
- Alfalfa
- Broccoli
- Fenugreek
- Radish

Bean, Pea, Grain And Legume Sprouts (Jars or Sprout Bags)

- Red, green and brown lentils
- Chick Peas (Garbanzo)
- Green Pea
- Aduki Beans
- Mung beans
- Buckwheat groats
- Quinoa

Grasses, Greens And Microgreens (Soil)

- Wheatgrass
- Sunflower greens
- Buckwheat lettuce
- Pea sprouts
- Broccoli

Everyone loves sprouts!

Our Wonderful World Media & Entertainment, Inc.
The Art of Living Green

We are a cutting-edge digital publishing company dedicated to helping all of us to live healthier, happier, greener lives that bring us into harmony with each other and our beautiful planet. Every day you'll find brilliant sustainable living ideas along with interesting information about improving your health, getting fit, refreshing your spirituality, achieving work-life balance and enhancing serenity. Then again, you'll also get the very latest in energy conservation tips, natural skincare, herbal and organic recipes, upcoming "green" events… and a whole lot more.

In addition to maintaining a dynamic interactive website at

www.owwmedia.com

We also provide the following products and services:

- e-Magazines
- e-Newsletters
- e-Brochures
- e-Blasts/Press Releases
- Feature Stories

- Book Design
- Streaming/Embedded Video
- Concert Production/Promotion
- Hardcopy Design Services
- And so much more!

For more info, please contact Glenn Swift at (772) 323-6925 or e-mail glenn@owwmedia.com.